SMALL
MISTAKES,
BIG
CONSEQUENCES

A personal and professional development guide

SMALL MISTAKES, BIG CONSEQUENCES

Develop Your Soft Skills to Help You Succeed

Discover 16 personality types you need to know

Anne Corley Baum
An Experienced Senior Executive with
a Witty Sense of Business Savvy

© 2018 by Anne Corley Baum

This publication also includes references to third-party trademarks, which are owned and may be registered by third parties whose products are reviewed in this publication.

Any and all unauthorized uses of these third-party marks are also prohibited.

Internet addresses given in this book were accurate at the time it went to press.

Printed in the United States of America

Cover and interior design and illustrations by Jennifer Giandomenico

Library of Congress information available upon request

ISBN 978-1-7323016-2-7

2   4   6   8   10   9   7   5   3   paperback

This guide is dedicated to my guardian angels in heaven: Elmer Gates, my dear friend and mentor, and my dad, Dr. W. Gene Corley who taught me, right from the start, that behavior matters. And to my awesome family—Brad, Reed, and Shay Baum, and my mom, Lynd Corley—thanks for always supporting me and my crazy ideas.

Contents

Introduction

When I sat down to write this book, my goal was to share common small mistakes that many people make that prevent them from being successful. Every day we interact with other people, yet we rarely think about our body language and behavior and, more importantly, the impact these behaviors have on how we are perceived by others.

Whether we like it or not and whether it is fair or not, perception is reality. People make subconscious decisions about who we are and our credibility the instant they see us. With that fact in mind, what can you do to have your perception equal *your* reality? How can you make the very best first, second, and ongoing impression on those with whom you interact?

First and foremost, we actually have to pay attention to how we act. From body language to the words we use, it is important to think about behavior as much as, if not more than, the business at hand. In practice, we tend to focus on data, presentation, and the technical side of an interaction instead of on our behavior.

Nothing you will read here is rocket science, and most of it you've probably heard in some form or fashion from mentors, parents, teachers, and advisors. The key for success with this guide is to put behavior at the top of your mind, then practice,

practice, and practice again. As you do so, these behaviors will become habit, and these habits will prevent you from making those small mistakes that result in big consequences. Remember that behavior is not a substitute for technical knowledge—you must know your facts and data to build credibility, and you must *always* operate with integrity—but you have a much better chance of having people trust your information and data when you avoid these small mistakes.

Enjoy!

> *Good is the enemy of great.*
> *—Jim Collins*

Small Mistake Number One

The Transmitter

The Transmitter is the person who is always talking, usually about himself and his accomplishments (or lack thereof). The Transmitter does not listen and is so focused on impressing you that you will rarely get a word into the conversation.

The Big Consequence

The Transmitter lives in an isolated world surrounded by his own perception of things. The Transmitter never knows where others stand on the issues and is rarely able to deliver what a client is looking to receive because he doesn't know their viewpoints. The Transmitter tends to be opinionated and never listens to other perspectives.

The Solutions

How to Avoid Being a Transmitter

Be a great listener. One tip that always helps is sharing that *listen* and *silent* have the same letters. This is a great way to remember that, in order to be a great listener, you actually have to be quiet! While listening to someone, make excellent eye contact and pay attention to what they are saying. You will learn a great deal about the person and what motivates them, and you will also be perceived as sincere and trustworthy—great characteristics to which we all should aspire.

How to Manage a Transmitter

When you meet a Transmitter, try to listen carefully to what he is saying and link your ideas, thoughts, and business opportunities with things that appear to be important to him. In some cases, you may need to ask the Transmitter to listen to you. Let him know how what you have to offer will help him succeed. (You can determine what he is trying to accomplish by asking.) This is not always a good strategy with a new acquaintance, but it's necessary with someone with whom you have to communicate on a regular basis.

How to Work with a Transmitter

Have patience when working with a Transmitter. They often don't realize that they are not listening and are actually trying to help. Starting a conversation with an introduction such as, "I'd like you to listen to my whole story before you offer any suggestions, and then I'd be happy to hear your opinion" can help. Most Transmitters are not trying to overwhelm the other person. They are just striving to be relevant.

> *We have two ears and one mouth so that we can listen twice as much as we speak.*
> *—Epictetus*

Small Mistake Number Two

The Solver

The Solver is always in rescue mode. When you approach the Solver with a problem, she immediately jumps in to start

working on the solution, often before she has even heard the entire issue. The Solver likes to show off her connections by picking up the phone or emailing someone right away.

The Big Consequence

By jumping in immediately, the Solver risks losing a number of leadership advantages:

- Taking on the problems of others allows for team members to dump their problems on the Solver, creating more work for the Solver and ending empowerment of the team.

- By doing, not teaching, the Solver is destined to continue to have to support the team. They will become dependent instead of independent, and the culture of the organization will decline.

- The Solver may be solving the wrong problem! By jumping in before understanding the full request, the Solver hasn't grasped the entire situation and may cause more issues.

The Solutions
How to Avoid Being a Solver

Empower your team. Empowerment requires three key elements:

- Trust
- Training and resources
- Coaching

When faced with questions from team members, ask them to explain what they think should be done. More often than not, they know exactly what to do, and they are looking for reassurance that they are headed in the right direction. Sometimes, they need additional assistance. When you help them find their own solution to a problem and train them to do it themselves, they will become more confident and will deliver a better product each and every time.

When I first got my driver's license, I always asked my dad for directions. Every time I asked, he pulled out the map—or sent me to get it—and taught me to find my way *on my own*. This simple lesson served me well and created a very independent mindset for me. Trust your team, help them learn how to do things, and coach them through the good and the bad. Remember that every mistake is a joint mistake. They need to be confident that you won't throw them under the bus. If you cut them off at the knees when they make a mistake—and *they* will—empowerment is dead in your organization. Believe in your team and make sure they know you have their back, and they will amaze you with their accomplishments.

How to Manage a Solver

If the Solver reports to you, have a talk with her about empowerment and the development of the team. Often, the Solver believes that it is her job to solve problems for the entire team. Teaching her the skills of empowerment will make her life easier and will create a stronger team.

How to Work with a Solver

Listen to the advice Solvers offer and let them know that they don't need to make the call or solve the issue for you. Tell them that you've got it and you appreciate their advice. When they can make a connection that you would otherwise not have, ask for the introduction and then take the lead in working with the other person to get the problem resolved on your own.

If you report to a Solver, come to her with solutions as well as problems. Ask her advice, but make it clear that you will run with the solution. This will help her build confidence in you.

> *Give me a fish and I eat for a day. Teach me to fish and I eat for a lifetime.*
> *—Chinese Proverb*

Small Mistake Number Three

The Front-of-Shirt Presser

The Front-of-Shirt Presser is the person who does just enough to get by from an appearance perspective. The Front-of-Shirt Presser irons only the part of his shirt that shows under the jacket; the back and sleeves are still wrinkled. He uses safety

pins to attach buttons, tapes falling hems, and hides stains under his jacket.

The Big Consequence

Unpolished is unpolished. Safety pins show, runs get longer, tape falls off, and the day will come when you will be forced to remove your jacket in a sweltering meeting room, revealing the partially pressed shirt. Getting caught with rigged fixes is almost worse than the original problem and hints that you are willing to take the easy way to solve a problem as opposed to getting to the root of the problem and fixing it correctly.

The Solutions

How to Avoid Being a Front-of-Shirt Presser

Be polished. Don't take the easy road. Image and perception begin with your appearance, so don't let your shortcuts get you in trouble. Polish shows, and it sends a message that quality is important to you. If people perceive that you prefer high quality, they will assume that the work you perform will be of a high quality. Sew on your buttons. Iron the whole shirt. Hire a tailor. Use a detergent pen. These extra steps will reflect well on your image, and your reputation as someone who delivers high quality will grow.

How to Manage a Front-of-Shirt Presser

Does this person work with you? Does he present himself to your clients? If so, you need to have a heart-to-heart conversation right away. Your organization is only as strong as the weakest person. If your team members are not presenting a polished image, then your company will not be perceived as such. Teaching your team to be polished helps everyone. If you need help, find a local store or person that specializes in professional attire and invite them in to teach your team.

How to Work with a Front-of-Shirt Presser

Your co-workers represent the company just as you do, so it is important to set the example and hold others accountable to the image you are striving to present for your company. Deal with image right from the start, define your expectations, and hold fast to those standards. Your company image is at stake, and it's important to teach your employees what your image is and how you'd like them to present themselves.

If you have a concern about a co-worker's presentation, you can speak to his supervisor or offer advice to the person directly. Image is very personal, and often people are put off by or uninterested in advice. Be kind in your approach and offer advice in the context of business success or company policy, not as personal criticism.

If this is your boss, you can offer advice and assistance like sharing your dry cleaner info, buying him a sewing kit, or sharing your tailor's contact info. Because the image of one reflects the image of all, you can also have a heart-to-heart conversation around dress code and presentation of the team.

Small Mistake Number Four

The Table Groomer

The Table Groomer has not learned the difference between a restroom and a dining table. The Table Groomer puts on lipstick

at the table, and she doesn't think twice about blowing her nose or brushing her hair while others are eating.

The Big Consequence

When one grooms at the table, others are forced to watch, and this distracts from the business at hand. This is particularly true with women in business. When others are focusing on lipstick or hair, they are not focusing on your intellect or message.

The Solutions

How to Avoid Being a Table Groomer

Excuse yourself. When dining at the corporate table, it is very important to keep the focus on the business that you plan to address. Avoid distractions by excusing yourself from the table or waiting until after the meeting to primp. Prepare yourself before the meeting begins; check the mirror to be sure that everything is in order—no food in the teeth, lipstick on, nose clear. Keep the meeting professional and focused. In doing so, no one will notice that your lipstick has faded or that your hair is askew.

How to Manage a Table Groomer

For members of your team, set the example and define expectations before you attend meetings. Explain why this behavior distracts from the result you are trying to achieve. If you observe this behavior with a customer or someone who is not on your team, invite them to join you in the restroom. You can set a good example and save them from the embarrassment at the table.

How to Work with a Table Groomer

Invite the Table Groomer to join you in the restroom as soon as you see her beginning to primp. Tempt her with the mirror and privacy. You can also speak to her about the distraction that table grooming creates.

> *No one needs to know how much, or how little, effort you put into presenting your fresh face to the world. Grooming is a behind-the-scenes activity; such matters should not be taken care of in public.*
> *—Jodi R. R. Smith*

Small Mistake Number Five

The Moocher

The Moocher never has his wallet. (He'll buy next time.) He always calls to request the free ticket. The Moocher calculates

his portion of a shared bill to the penny and rarely offers to contribute to charitable causes and organizations.

The Big Consequence

Over time, the Moocher gains the reputation of being selfish or greedy. He is often viewed as a freeloader. This is especially true when the Moocher has a significant income stream. Invitations stop coming, and jokes are made. People judge the Moocher's work product and company by his actions and choose to do business elsewhere.

The Solutions

How to Avoid Being a Moocher

Be generous. Give more than you get. Generosity is one of the greatest characteristics that one can possess. Think of it as "the favor" bank—a bank into which you always make deposits and never make a withdrawal.

The favors will be returned to you in many ways, usually linked indirectly to the favors that have been done for others. When you invite someone to dine with you, it is your responsibility to pay. When you have the chance to donate to a charitable organization, do so, even if it is a small amount of money. Treat people to events. Send thank-you notes and gifts. Appreciate what others do for you, and they'll appreciate you in the long run.

Be remembered for your good deeds. Work and business success provide the means, and heart provides the drive. Give back, be generous, but do so sincerely. You will receive great dividends from the most unlikely sources.

How to Manage a Moocher

Teach philanthropy. Not everyone learned generosity and philanthropy as they were growing up. It is an important skill set to teach others. Provide employees and colleagues with the opportunity to lead by giving of their time, talent, and treasure. Not everyone will follow suit, but many will.

How to Work with a Moocher

When you work with a Moocher, let him know the payment arrangements before you go to any meal. Collect money up front for tickets or group gifts. Try connecting him to a mission when you are encouraging him to donate to a good cause.

Try to find out what motivates the Moocher and invite him to get involved. Sometimes, people are simply ignorant of giving. Not everyone is raised with the notion of philanthropy, and teaching someone to be generous is one of the greatest gifts you can give. On the other hand, some people are just greedy or selfish. You don't have to take them to lunch or give them tickets. Spend your time with other generous people. You will be surprised how happy those encounters will be.

Small Mistake Number Six

The Celebrity

The Celebrity thinks that everyone knows her. This person fails to introduce herself. She will often say things like, "You

don't remember me, do you?" This person tends to get angry when she is not remembered and presents an aggravated or arrogant approach to all.

The Big Consequence

Failing to introduce yourself makes others uncomfortable. As much as people would like to remember everyone, they often do not. This is especially true when they see someone out of context, such as seeing a physician outside of the hospital or a teacher outside of a school.

The Solutions

How to Avoid Being a Celebrity

Be friendly. Introduce yourself—always. It never hurts to introduce yourself and shake hands with a colleague. Offering your company name or where they might remember you adds to the introduction. When you introduce yourself, you put others at ease, and you present an air of confidence. People like doing business with friendly people, and they appreciate it when you put them at ease by introducing yourself and saving them from the agony of trying to place you. Courtesy counts, and the person who introduces herself regularly is more well known and respected for having done so.

Success is based on who you know, but even more importantly on who knows you. If you introduce yourself regularly, your network will grow along with your reputation.

How to Manage a Celebrity

If a Celebrity works for you, model non-celeb behavior to her. Introduce yourself. Be confident but not cocky. If you have to, gently explain that sometimes she comes off as brash, when she probably means to be confident.

How to Work with a Celebrity

When confronted with the Celebrity's arrogance, simply ask her to tell you who she is and where you might last have met. I always add in a confident statement, for example, "I know we've met, you look familiar, but I can't place you. Please remind me where we've met." By the way, it is a great skill to remember names; try to do so whenever possible. The Celebrity's behavior is no excuse not to be mindful of names—just an annoying habit that some people use to put you in an uncomfortable position.

> *Being humble means recognizing that we are not on earth to see how important we can become, but to see how much difference we can make in the lives of others.*
> *—Gordon B. Hinchey*

Small Mistake Number Seven

The Blamer

The Blamer never makes mistakes; it is always someone else's fault. In many cases, the Blamer has already thought out who to blame creating various scenarios that exonerate him before

anyone has discovered that there is a problem. The Blamer is the first to know that he is responsible and the very last to admit it.

The Big Consequence

Over time, lack of accountability and pointing the finger catches up with you. Supervisors lose trust and respect for you. Peers will not support you and will wonder when management will remove you from your job. If leadership is not quick to hold the Blamer accountable, the rest of the team will start to wonder why they should work so hard to achieve success when the Blamer continues to point the finger and get away with not carrying his share of the load.

The Solutions

How to Avoid Being a Blamer

Be accountable for your actions. No one is perfect. I'll say it again: *No one* is perfect. Mistakes are the way we learn. *Every mistake is tuition.* Though it is critically important to learn lessons from mistakes and do your best not to repeat them, it is far better to be accountable for your actions than to try to point fingers at others. Act with integrity. Own up to your mistakes and learn from them. You will be more successful in the long run and will earn the respect of your colleagues. Respect is a great reward to gain and one worth working toward.

How to Manage a Blamer

When an employee is not taking ownership, you need to show him:

(1) That you have his back and will coach him through the situation. There is nothing more powerful than supporting your employees when something goes wrong.

(2) How to take ownership by owning your own mistakes and being humble. There is a fine line between mistakes that are learning experiences and those that are performance issues. If you see the same mistake over and over again from one individual, that is a performance issue that requires disciplinary action.

How to Work with a Blamer

Do everything that you can to hold yourself and others accountable. If the Blamer works with you, don't let him use excuses for not getting the job finished. Hold him accountable for his actions. Practice open, honest two-way communication regularly. You will be surprised how many people will stop blaming and start doing when they are held accountable and take ownership of their responsibilities.

Small Mistake Number Eight

The Smart Phone Checker

The Smart Phone Checker is always checking to see who called, texted, or emailed. This person is addicted to eCommunication and can't wait to see who "needs" her. The Smart Phone Checker often places her device of choice on a table or desk, in

full view, and sets it to vibrate. (Or worse, she leaves the ringer turned on to some catchy Top 40 tune that represents who she is when she's not working.)

The Smart Phone Checker will glance at her device throughout a meeting, often with no apology. She will sometimes read texts and emails while talking and often say things like, "I'm listening to you, please continue" or burst out laughing at the hilarious inside joke that she just read. Sometimes, she will even answer the phone in the middle of your conversation.

The Big Consequence

Every time the Smart Phone Checker checks her device, she is sending the message to others that the caller/texter is more important than the person in the room. Though many of us pride ourselves on our ability to multitask, it is impossible to really listen to another person while reading texts and email or checking to see who is calling. It is a huge distraction and undermines trust and respect in the relationship.

The Solutions

How to Avoid Being a Smart Phone Checker

Be present. **Turn off the device.** Put it in your briefcase, bag, or portfolio. Offer your full attention to those with whom you are meeting. They have taken time out of their day to dedicate to you, so offer them the same courtesy. The world will not end if you return a call, text, or email in an hour or two—*after the meeting.*

In the event there is the rare true emergency interruption, explain it to the people with whom you are meeting. If you know beforehand, give them the "heads up" if you anticipate an issue and explain your need to take a call, emphasizing that your time with your guests is the priority.

How to Manage a Smart Phone Checker

Setting a great example sends a message. When I know that I am meeting with someone who is addicted to her device, I will often make a point of turning off my device and putting it away in front of the Smart Phone Checker, sending a message through action.

For team members, make this part of your culture and practice. Explain the need to respect the time and attention of others and give your team the tools to be well received by all.

How to Work with a Smart Phone Checker

Set up rules of engagement for meetings. Establish a no-cell-phone policy and ask everyone to put phones away for meetings that you are leading. Provide a basket for depositing phones before the meeting. Not only will you gain the full attention of the participants; your meetings will be more efficient, productive, and shorter. It will keep everyone focused and present.

Small Mistake Number Nine

The Wandering Eye

There are two species of the Wandering Eye. The first likes to look colleagues up and down, checking out every inch of their body from head to toe and in between. The second won't

make eye contact in any way, looking away as soon as he shakes hands and scanning the crowd for a friendly face while pretending to engage in conversation with a colleague.

The Big Consequence

Both Wandering Eye behaviors are disrespectful. Period.

The Wandering Eye #1: Need I say more? The instant that someone begins to check out anything below the chin—whether it is an ugly outfit or a voluptuous figure, the tone of the interaction jumps from business to social. The person being "checked out" is immediately uncomfortable, and the person doing the checking is perceived as rude and inappropriate and often even creepy.

The Wandering Eye #2: This Wandering Eye sends a message of disrespect to the person with whom he is interacting as well as a message of low self-confidence. When someone appears to be shifty eyed, the other person perceives him to be untrustworthy or up to something.

The Solutions
How to Avoid Being a Wandering Eye

Focus your attention in the eyes of the person with whom you are communicating. This is the only place to look when you are conducting business, and it sends a message of trust and confidence. Be careful not to overdo eye contact and stare at people. This makes people feel uncomfortable.

If you are uncomfortable looking someone in the eye or if it is difficult to do so because of their actions, focus on the safe zone, between the eyes, just above the nose. It will look as if you are looking the person directly in the eye!

How to Manage a Wandering Eye

If someone who works with you has issues with his (or her!) focus, talk to him and explain that even though he might think the person he is checking out doesn't notice, they *always* do. You cannot sneak a look and think the other person won't notice. Coaching about appropriate behavior is key. Let your team know what is acceptable and unacceptable behavior so they understand your expectations and the image the company is trying to portray.

How to Work with a Wandering Eye

Always keep the conversations focused on business and the subject at hand. Sit at a table or desk to keep the focus on the subject of the business, not what you're wearing.

If someone is always checking you out, consider how you dress and be sure to keep your work outfits professional.

> *Important note: Eye contact is cultural, so make sure you study the cultural norms before traveling abroad for business to avoid eye contact missteps.*

Small Mistake Number 10

The Spin Doctor

The Spin Doctor alters the truth to fit the situation. From leaving out key information to directly altering a story, the Spin Doctor carefully chooses her words to communicate only as much of the truth as she deems necessary to succeed. Some

Hmm... How can I twist this to get what I want?

Spin Doctors will flat out lie to get what they want, and they are very good at it, so it is often not obvious or easily verifiable.

The Big Consequence

Someone who has the reputation as a Spin Doctor is not trusted or respected. It is incredibly difficult to recover from a loss of trust and respect. Often, it's impossible.

The Solutions

How to Avoid Being a Spin Doctor

Always act with integrity. Integrity and honesty are the most important attributes of any individual. When one acts with integrity, it is never necessary to remember which version of the story was told. When one draws from the truth, it is easy to keep the story straight. When you operate in an open, honest manner, you always know the right version of the story! And you build trust with everyone you encounter.

How to Manage a Spin Doctor

Keep her accountable. If you catch someone in a spin, ask questions that get to the bottom line. Listen carefully to what she is saying and evaluate the information compared to the facts that you know. Ask questions. If you can't get to the truth or the whole story with someone regularly, do business with someone you can trust. Move on.

How to Work with a Spin Doctor

Call out the Spin Doctor when she starts to spin a story and keep the focus on the facts versus assumptions. If you know a person doesn't always tell the whole story, ask clarifying questions to get the full story on the table. Don't assume that she's given you all the information you need. Probe and verify before taking action.

> *With integrity, you have nothing to fear since you have nothing to hide.* —*Zig Ziglar*

Small Mistake Number 11

The Professor

The Professor knows it all and wants you to know that he does. No matter what the topic, the Professor has an opinion—the right and the only opinion. He does not wish to discuss, debate, or even hear your opinion, regardless of your expertise on the subject. He often interrupts and monopolizes a discussion.

The Big Consequence

People do not like to feel inferior. When a person acts like they know it all, and particularly when he does so in a way that insults the other person, it is unlikely that a strong bond or relationship will be built.

Projecting an image of "knowing it all" also sends a message that the speaker lacks self-confidence. People prefer to do business with people who are confident in themselves. The Professor projects arrogance and elitism, not confidence.

The Solutions

How to Avoid Being a Professor

Listen up. Speak respectfully and listen to the opinions of others and offer your opinions in a constructive manner. Avoid using "I know" or "I did." Let people finish their stories. Especially when someone is presenting a story, try not to flip it into a story about you. Participate in conversations; don't dominate them.

How to Manage a Professor

When dealing with the Professor, take his opinion and add your angle to it. For example, "I see your point. Have you ever heard of xyz?" Offering new information in a non-confrontational manner can open ears—and minds.

How to Work with a Professor

If a Professor is a colleague, and you often have confrontational meetings, sit down and discuss the issue. Often the Professor doesn't realize that he is behaving in an arrogant or confrontational manner. Be assertive in presenting your position and encourage him to listen to your perspective as well.

> *Wise men speak because they have something to say. Fools because they have to say something. —Plato*

Small Mistake Number 12

The Gossip

The Gossip loves to share juicy—usually nasty—stories about others. The gossip loves the phrases "just between you and me," "confidentially," and "I wouldn't say this to him, but …" Words like these are a tip-off that the conversation is headed in a bad

direction. The gossip loves to put others down to make herself look superior and, frankly, to make her feel better about herself.

The Gossip rarely shares her criticism with the target of her gossip. She often doesn't have the facts completely lined up or researched.

The Big Consequence

When you talk about other people behind their backs, the person with whom you are sharing the gossip wonders what you say about *them* to others. Gossip breaks down trust, and it leads to half-truths being spread like wildfire. And worst of all, it's mean.

The Solutions

How to Avoid Being a Gossip

Stop gossip and don't be drawn in. Humans are naturally curious. We are always intrigued by an interesting story, particularly one that presents bad news about otherwise good or successful people. Consider how popular celebrity gossip magazines and news shows are in the United States. Most of us like to know the bad side of successful people so we can feel better about ourselves. Don't be drawn in!

Don't assume the worst about people, and certainly don't continue to pass on the information unless you personally know it to be true. Even then, passing the information on may not be the right thing to do. If passing on the information hurts someone unnecessarily, don't do it. You wouldn't want someone to do it to you. You look petty when you do pass on negative gossip.

By the way, all bets are off on this one if you know that criminal behavior has taken place. It is your duty to report or stop it, period.

How to Manage a Gossip

Stop gossip before it starts. When one of your team members comes to you with gossip, quickly shift any discussions to business-related impacts. If the person is there just to spread nasty rumors, steer her away from gossip by driving the conversation back to the business at hand.

How to Work with a Gossip

As tempting as it may be, don't pile on and become the Gossip yourself. When someone presents you with gossip and tries to draw you in, answer by saying, "Wow, if I had time to deal with everyone else's problems, I'd be lucky" or "I hadn't heard about that, but you're here to talk about business. How can I help?" When you defer gossip, people get the hint and stop.

If someone is particularly persistent, just let her know that you prefer to talk *to* people, not *about* them.

Small Mistake Number 13

The Empty Promiser

The Empty Promiser loves to offer his services, money, or solutions, yet he rarely delivers on that which he has prom-

ised. The Empty Promiser, at first, seems very helpful. People are often touched by his willingness to lend a hand, contribute, or drive a solution. However, the Empty Promiser is big on offers and short on delivery. The check never comes, the excuses expand, and the solutions are never found.

It is important to note that many Empty Promisers are *well intentioned*, but disorganized or forgetful. Most people really mean to be helpful, but if they do not keep a note on what they promised, the risks are significant.

The Big Consequence

The Empty Promiser leaves a trail of disappointment. The positive initial first impression is quickly worn away, and people don't trust the Empty Promiser anymore. This lack of trust is not limited to the promises made but not kept. It extends to all activities of the person and causes a severely damaged reputation.

The Solutions

How to Avoid Being an Empty Promiser

Deliver. If you promise to do something, do it and do it right away. Keep notes on what you've promised to whom. Surprise people with a quick response. Don't make them wait or, worse, ask again because often they never will. Keeping promises and delivering *before expected* sets one up to be highly admired, valued, and deserving trust. These are great characteristics for success.

How to Manage an Empty Promiser

Remind him! If you really would like something that was promised, ask for it. I like to go with the "three strikes" rule. If you ask three times and nothing happens, move on. Most of the time, the person will respond, apologetically, when reminded.

For your team, build a culture that is responsive. Deliver on promises and make it easy for people to work with you and your team. If you make a mistake, apologize, learn from it, and move forward.

How to Work with an Empty Promiser

When someone promises to do something, it's great to recap deliverables and due dates at the end of a meeting. When you work with someone who forgets what he promised to do, it's perfectly acceptable to follow up and ask him for what it is that he promised. If someone reminds you, don't be angry, and get the job done.

Small Mistake Number 14

The Wimpy or Tough Handshaker

The Wimpy Handshaker is so afraid of hurting another person, or so unsure of the correct manner or timing of a handshake,

that she ends up delivering a limp, ineffective handshake.

The Tough Handshaker wants to be sure to deliver such a firm handshake that the handshake leaves the other party grimacing in pain and wishing the other person would lighten up.

The Big Consequence

In business, the primary contact that you have with another person comes through the handshake. The person who extends their hand first in a conversation demonstrates confidence, and they put the other person at ease.

When you offer a wimpy handshake, people *perceive* that you are weak and lack confidence.

When you offer a tough handshake, people *perceive* you as arrogant, overconfident, or cocky.

The Solutions

How to Avoid Being a Wimpy/Tough Handshaker

Work on your handshake. Learn to shake hands correctly and adjust your handshake style to the situation at hand. Be prepared to shake hands with everyone you meet and to do so with confidence. Don't over- or underdo the shake. Be brief, firm, and solid in your handshake. Always make eye contact, smile, and introduce yourself. You will be amazed at the results!

How to Manage a Wimpy/Tough Hand-shaker

Work on handshakes with her and give her the tools to succeed. She will thank you and represent you and your company well. Teach her how to control her grip with her fingertips and not to be afraid of a firm shake.

How to Work with a Wimpy/Tough Hand-shaker

Don't let her see your reaction! This is the most important part of the handshake. Even if you sense that a person is under- or overdoing her handshake, continue with your shake and move on to the business at hand.

Don't make assumptions about the person's character or style based on their handshake. Judge her for her intellect, personality, and inherent value.

Always strive to put another person at ease, even when she doesn't shake hands correctly. Go with the flow!

Small Mistake Number 15

The eRanter

The eRanter likes to use email, texting, or social media to share his anger and frustrations. The eRanter loves to write in

all caps to show that he is yelling. He is generally passive-aggressive and often will rant about people to others instead of speaking directly to the person in question.

The Big Consequence

There are two big consequences.

- Once anything leaves your computer or phone, you lose control over what happens to it. It can be forwarded, printed, or posted on the Internet, reflecting poorly on you, your style, and your company.

- People don't appreciate being assaulted via email or text. There is no tone associated with eCommunication, so your tone and purpose are left to the interpretation of the reader. This can lead to misinterpretation and misunderstandings.

The Solutions

How to Avoid Being an eRanter

Have courage and communicate. If you have an issue with someone, speak to him face-to-face. Be open and honest. Listen to what he has to say. When you nip an issue in the bud, it is often easily resolved. Letting things simmer and using email and texts for arguments, discipline, or telling someone what you "really think of them" rarely succeeds. It ruins relationships.

You should never post or send anything that you don't

want forwarded, printed, or seen in the public forum or in a court of law. Once you send it, you've lost control, so make sure that everything you send represents you well.

How to Manage an eRanter

Speak to him in person, directly and right away. Be clear on appropriate format, style, and wording. Do not allow it to continue. There is risk to relationships internally and externally. One poor email can create a lot of problems.

How to Work with an eRanter

If someone is sending you ranting emails or texts, first, resist the urge to respond in kind—be careful not to turn into an eRanter in responding to one!

Second, request a meeting or phone conversation. Though it is hard at first, dealing with issues directly and face-to-face always works out better in the long run.

Because an eRanter may also be passive-aggressive in his style, he may not agree to meet with you. If that's the case, move on and ask him to call or meet with you in the future if he has an issue. Let him know that you are always open to discussion of any issues, but not via email or text.

Small Mistake Number 16

The Name Dropper

The Name Dropper wants everyone to know who she knows. She is always using the names of famous people to justify her

position in society, yet she often does not have a true connection with the people to whom she refers.

The Name Dropper often carries an air of superiority or arrogance associated with her real or professed connection to famous or well-known people.

The Big Consequence

Unfortunately, the Name Dropper is often perceived as a bragger or arrogant. When it becomes clear that her association with the people she pretends to know does not pan out, her credibility is tarnished.

This impacts the perception of the Name Dropper's integrity, and name dropping also takes away from the credibility of the individual themselves. Why deal with this person, if you can deal with the source directly?

The Solutions

How to Avoid Being a Name Dropper

Be yourself. Define yourself for who you are and what you believe. Using the reputation of others to substantiate who you are and what you believe doesn't establish a reputation for *you*. And often, name dropping is misunderstood to be showing off, bragging, or talking down to those with whom you interact. These are characteristics that do not lend themselves to building strong, solid, and long-lasting relationships.

How to Manage a Name Dropper

Asking the Name Dropper what she personally believes will, over time, help her see her individual value. If she reports to you, explain to her the consequences of name dropping and help her to see when the behavior is demonstrated. Build her confidence and help her see the value she brings to the organization.

How to Work with a Name Dropper

When working with Name Droppers, move the conversation to the business at hand and don't be distracted by the references. Show them their value as team members and help them to see their own worth.

> *To help yourself, you must be yourself. Be the best that you can be. When you make a mistake, learn from it, pick yourself up, and move on. —Dave Pelzer*

Strategies for Success

Quick Tips to Help Keep You on Track

1) Be a great listener.
2) Empower your team.
3) Be polished; don't take the easy road.
4) Excuse yourself.
5) Be generous. Give more than you get.
6) Be friendly. Introduce yourself, always.
7) Be accountable for your actions.
8) Be present. Turn off your device.
9) Focus your attention in the eyes of the person with whom you are communicating.
10) Always act with integrity.
11) Speak respectfully and listen to the opinions of others.
12) Stop gossip and don't be drawn in.
13) Deliver.
14) Work on your handshake.
15) Have courage and communicate.
16) Be yourself.

Acknowledgments

There are many people to thank for the wisdom and observations that led to the creation of these characters and the solutions to avoid them:

Elmer Gates, Mike Caruso, Martin Till, Tony Iannelli, Rick Anderson, Lee Butz, Tony Salvaggio, Jack Pfunder, Todd Welch, Bonnie Hagemann, Michelle Griffin Young, Danielle Joseph, Drea Rosko, Chrissy Hixson, Sally Gammon, Buddy Lesavoy, Dorothea Johnson, Francis Hesselbein, Kostas Kalogeropoulos, Ilene Hochberg Wood, Kim Howie, Nancy Werteen, Shelley Redding, Michelle Landis, Laurie Hackett, Dr. Sam Giamber, and of course, my family: Lynd, Gene, Bob, Chris, Scott and Melissa Corley, Libby Lenz, the Wertheims, the Baum/Hickmott/Perlin Crew, and most importantly Brad, Reed, and Shay Baum.

Special thanks to Jessie Seneca for lighting a fire under my chair and to Anne Alexander and Jennifer Reich for believing in the concept.

About the Author

Anne Corley Baum is the Lehigh Valley executive and vice president, distribution channels and labor relations for Capital BlueCross. She is the senior leader in the Capital BlueCross Lehigh Valley office. Anne leads the network of more than 5,500 producers, and she's responsible for the plan's organized labor customers.

Since joining the company in January 2010, Anne has been involved with strategic planning, operations, partnership development, community relations, corporate giving, sales, and account management throughout Capital BlueCross' eastern service area.

Anne is the owner of Vision Accomplished, a firm dedicated to leadership and culture. Anne is active in the community and has served in leadership roles with many boards and executive committees.

In 2003 Anne was selected as one of the Best 50 Women in PA Business. Anne received the Lehigh Valley SUITS award in 2009, and she was selected by the Leukemia and Lymphoma Society as Woman of the Year in 2010. She received the Girl Scout's Take the Lead Award and the Chamber Woman's Business Council ATHENA Award in 2013. In 2015, she was named as a Woman of Influence by Lehigh Valley Business. In April 2017, Anne received the Golden Laurel Award from the YWCA of Bethlehem.

A native of Glenview, IL, Anne holds a BS in Biology from the University of Illinois, Champaign-Urbana, IL, and an MS in Health Systems Management from Rush University, Chicago, IL. She is certified by the Protocol School of Washington as a protocol and etiquette consultant.

She is a proud mother of two wonderful children and is married to her high school sweetheart.

Coming soon from Vision Accomplished and Momosa Publishing:

Small Mistakes, Big Consequences for Conference Calls
Small Mistakes, Big Consequences for Interviews
Small Mistakes, Big Consequences for College